WHAT OTHER PE(

"I believe that personal responsibility is a key to success in any area of ...
John Buchanan shows us all that this extends to our personal relationships.
Instead of trying to find the right person, we can proactively take steps to be the
right person."

Jim Stovall
President, Narrative Television Network
Author, The Ultimate Gift

John Buchanan has not written just a 'book', but a practical lifestyle program
designed to give men of all ages the opportunity to examine their own daily living
habits and their attitudes toward the women in their world. Here, in a comfort-
able setting, the 'gentlemen' is guided in his communication that will help him
better understand and treat the 'lady' in his life. It is based on the belief that the
courtship and marriage relationship is the most significant of all relationships.

Dr. Mark Maynard,
Radio Host, "Adventures of Christian Entrepreneurs"
and Professor of Business, Evangel University.

"John Buchanan intentionally and effectively challenges the reader to have
a teachable spirit to purposefully develop outright integrity, courtesy and
etiquette in order to be positively presentable and pleasantly acceptable. No
manipulative or exploitive tactics will win a genuinely respectable lady's hand
or heart. In order to become "Mr. Right", that man must cultivate qualities of
genuine respect, sincere appreciation, and servant leadership with a listening
ear. *His clean heart AND PURE CONSCIENCE* will communicate his presentable and acceptable identity. With meticulous observations and personal experience, the author has ingeniously created a fundamental manual for healthy,
successful, and lasting relationships."

Dr. Joseph B. Mukasa
B.A. Honors (English) B.A. High Honors (Min. Arts)
M.A. (Theatre Arts) M.Div., M.A. (Bib. Lit.)
Ph.D. (Dramatic Art)
Assistant Professor of Communication, Oral Roberts University
President, COTEAM, INC.
Co-Founder and Advisor , Good Shepherd Children's Home,
(an Orphanage Project sponsored by COTEAM in Uganda, East Africa)

God Bless You!

BE *Perfect* FOR HER

A Biblical Approach to Becoming the RIGHT ONE

JOHN BUCHANAN JR.

Be Perfect for Her
A Biblical Approach to Becoming the RIGHT ONE

ISBN 0-88144-345-X
Copyright © 2008 by John G. Buchanan, Jr.

Published by
Total Publishing and Media
7707 East 111th Street South, Suite 104
Tulsa, Oklahoma 74133

This book is dedicated to Faith,
without her this book would not have been possible—
Thank You for being *Perfect for Me!*

Acknowledgements

I would first and foremost like to thank my Risen Lord Jesus Christ—He *is* the reason.

Second, I would like to thank my sweetheart Faith, she is my motivation. My parents and sisters deserve a great deal of gratitude for putting up with me since birth. Leland Terry, you have been a great source of encouragement and a help in troubled times. Jerry Williams has taught me so much—mainly how to listen—Thanks Jerry. All of my teachers throughout Victory Bible Institute, as well as Oral Roberts University—I can think of no better institutions in the world. Dick Knox at Mounds First Baptist Church and Dr. Joseph Mukasa at ORU—Thank you for teaching me the love of God! Also, a great deal of thanks to Mounds Public Schools and their encouragement throughout my childhood. A special thank you to T.L. Osborn. In my first year of VBI, you looked at me (I was running the camera) and said God Believes in You—You will not know the impact that statement has had on my life until eternity—I am sure Daisy knows. The love that the two of you share has impacted my life. Billy Joe Daugherty, for looking me in the eye and speaking the truth. Dr. Mark Maynard, we did it! Jim Stovall, for teaching us about giving. Jana Christian at the Oklahoma School of Etiquette for tips on etiquette And last but not least, all of the ladies out there that have let me listen to you and taught me what God wants in a man—Thank You!

Also one last very special thank you to David Salustri, who did an amazing job on the cover art. David you're a genius!

If you would like to contact David, please email him at:

daveinpublic@aol.com

Contents

Preface

I think every man should know how to treat a lady. However, we live in a selfish, self-seeking, self-fulfilling society where we are taught from birth that it is all about Me!

This path of thinking has lead to the Post-Moral society we now live in. One where divorce, promiscuity, uncouthness, and animal like behavior controls us, because we live by an instinct from birth that tells us "If it feels good do it".

I am here to tell you that the cross that Jesus Christ bore for us did not "feel good".

But *Nothing* else in history has ever brought such good!

Gentlemen, let's take up our cross and follow after our Lord Jesus by loving and respecting the women that He died for!

Introduction

This book comes from a heart that longs to see things become the way that God intended them to be. That is why I strive to use multiple Bible verses to illustrate what God has taught me over several years of studying the opposite gender. I have endured years of frustrations seeking to understand why women act as they do and how God could have made them—because in my mind they just don't make sense all the time. But that's just it. In my mind—not His! In His mind things are not the way that He originally created them to be. He originally designed man and his wife to be one. He did not design them to be two separate entities pursuing their own will, but rather two separate entities; jointly, in heart, mind, and spirit pursuing one will—*His!* I am seeking to get there. Would you join me?

I know that we can arrive back at the original state He created us to be in, because He made it possible through His Blood! I know it is doable, but we need to start with the head of the household—which is the husband (You, if not now—soon!)

Women hold a special place in God's heart. In God's original creation, they were the only being taken from another. In other words, God formed Adam from the dust and breathed life into him. To make a woman, God took a rib out of Adam and formed her. The funny thing is, is that we actually named her a woman. If you notice in Genesis, God did not name her a woman. I personally think it was a shortened version of WOW MAN! Look at her! He specifically created her for us. If your dad gave you a sports car that was worth hundreds of thousands of dollars—how would you treat it? You would treat it very well, wouldn't you? Look at it this way, God

(Creator of the Universe) gave you a fearfully and wonderfully made gift—paid for by the blood of His Son. How should you treat her? With that said, let's start a journey together with Him, in learning how to love and respect a woman.

With this book we are starting a process in you that will renew your mind and restore righteousness to your relationships, eventually ending at His Throne—hearing Him say, "Well Done, My Good and Faithful Servant."

CHAPTER 1

Grooming

Women like looks! This is a simple and profound statement—but true! Even God cares about grooming. If you need proof read the books of Exodus and Leviticus. God is not as concerned with the way you look on the outside as much as the way that you look on the inside, but it is worth noticing how He had His priests dress, especially when they came into the Holy of Holies in the Tabernacle. The priest would instantly die if he did not have everything perfect to what God required of him. We are New Testament priests according to 1 Peter 2:9.

> 1 Peter 2:9 "But you are a chosen people, a royal priesthood, a holy nation, a people belonging to God, that you may declare the praises of him who called you out of the darkness into his wonderful life." (NIV)

I am not saying that you have to have perfect grooming to find that right woman, but it's not going to hurt! Having said that, a woman will not be as interested in you if you are not properly groomed, her reasoning for this is that if you cannot take of yourself—you will not be able to take care of her. This is found in her need to find security and stability in you. She cannot see your heart until she knows you, so give her a reason to see your heart!

We think that our looks are not as important as other things and we are right in this. However, women look at things from a different perspective and this book is designed to help you reason out their thoughts. The way women view your appearance could be summed up in a simple statement. Looks are the paint job on the car. If you have ever watched a woman buy a car, they pace around it and sit down in the driver's seat and ask how they look. They want to feel secure in the car and they feel that if it looks like it is in great shape, it will be able to take care of them. We all understand that it's the engine that matters, however, you might have trouble selling it without a good paint job, because women are looking at the appearance of the car foremost, this is the exact same way they look at you! Another note on this—They are excellent shoppers!

Let's take a very logical look at this. You like the way women look. God understands this because He designed them specifically for us. God being the God He is, left them plenty of room to work with. They take this and run with it, some more than others. Women are creatures of habit, and these habits focus foremost on their looks. They will shop endlessly for the rest of their lives looking for the perfect outfit. They will find it, then, in a few days it will change and no longer be the perfect outfit. This is because women constantly assess how they look and in several different dimensions that we would never even think about. For example, the perfect eyelashes, eyebrows, eye shadow, eye contacts and color, eye shape, darkness or wrinkles under the eye, and it goes on. Now all of the things I listed are located in an area that could fit in the palm of your hand! I understand that they are not as specific with other areas of the body, but if they could be they would be!

If women put this amount of focus on their looks, they are going to expect effort on your part as well, whether it is conscious or unconscious. This is why we have to put some effort into our appearance, if we want girls to notice us.

There are all sorts of ways to improve your appearance. Hair is a great place to start! My girlfriend is a hairstylist, so I have a little insider information in this area. Some guys always look like they have great hair and the reason for this is that they have a great hair stylist and you need one, too! There are lots of great stylists out there; I have the best already (I date her!). Unless you are one of the very few guys that actually have an idea what the girls are looking for, you definitely need to have your hairstylist fix your hair the way that she wants. Remember that they went to school and received a certificate and license to do this.

I recommend that you find a hairstylist that works for herself, and yes I did say herself. Your best bet on a haircut that will attract the ladies, is going to come from a lady. There are definitely guys that can give good haircuts, but you want what the women want, and the odds are that the ladies are going to know what will look best on you. The reason I recommend a self-employed hairstylist is simple. They are going to give you the best hair cut you can get, because they want you to come back to them! A guy should get his hair cut preferably every 3-4 weeks, but definitely no longer than that. There are all sorts of things that girls look for in a guy's hair that we do not notice, and that is why I recommend this time frame.

The next area that should be addressed is proper clothing attire. This can be a very touchy subject for women because it all depends on your body type. Their reasoning for this is because they wear clothes based on their body type. A definite NO are tight pants and jeans. Admit it men, your posterior was designed for work, not shapeliness, so no tight jeans—period. From there it goes crazy and there are very few road maps, but I will give you all the tips I can. Always take a lady near your age shopping with you. This is your fail-safe; it is to help prevent you from wasting money on the wrong clothes.

The next thing is to dress your age. If you're in your younger twenties dress your age. However, from your upper twenties on, dressing your age means to typically dress five to ten years younger than what you are. If you are in your teens, this statement does not apply to you. Although women might find it cute if you dressed up as a 6 year old, they won't date you! An important note on this: different occasions require different attire.

There should be different designated clothes for different occasions. You should first and foremost have a pleasant casual set of clothes. These should be in good taste, but trendy. The present styles now for guys in their twenties are tight t-shirts and loose factory torn jeans. I know, you can buy the jeans and rip them yourselves—but don't; Somehow, some way, girls know the difference.

Your formal clothes should definitely be dress shirts, but stylish ones. The key to dress shirts is in the colors. White is always a great color! However, if you want to impress the ladies wear pink. You need to be careful with your pinks, though. Never go neon in any color, especially pink. Pastel colors seem to go over well with the ladies as well. Dark and light blue, green, and black are acceptable, too. This all depends upon the occasion though. If it is light-hearted, keep it light-hearted with lighter colors.

Shoes are extremely important. They are definitely noticed by the ladies, usually first. Buy in style shoes! Do not buy shoes because they are cool or you think that they look good. Once again make sure and have a lady's opinion when you buy shoes. You need to have at least five different pairs of shoes. They are: casual comfort (for everyday use), casual dress (usually a leather shoe), athletic (you can pick what you like on this one, for now), sandals or flip-flops, and a really classy dress shoe. You should only wear your athletic shoes when doing athletics. The other shoes are self-explanatory for the most part. Sandals are the exception. You can also wear these as a casual dress with jeans and a dress shirt, with a white t-shirt on underneath.

Also, keep plenty of white undershirts handy. These you can wear all the time and are very much appreciated by the lady folk. Just make sure that they are a brilliant white with no stains and are crisp! An important note is that white socks are definitely the same way, however never wear them when you are dressing up. Instead, buy a few pair of nice dress socks and were them instead.

Your pants are probably the easiest part of your wardrobe, with the exception of the white undershirts. Keep it simple. Blue jeans and tan khakis. Make sure that they are not tight or cheap. Women appreciate a good label on your pants, because it is visible to all other women and lets them know the status of the guy she is dating. You can venture into other colors of pants like white, black, or blue, but proceed very cautiously. These will need specific shirts and shoes to go along with them. The reason I say blue jeans and tan khakis is because they will go with any type of shirt and shoes you decide to wear. So keep it simple, because there are other things you need to spend your time on.

Coats are very simple too! Make sure and have two to three of them. You should have a nice cloth like coat and a leather jacket at least. Get rid of the old sports team coat, very few girls like these any more. Replace it with a jacket that she would like to wear. That's correct—one that she would like to wear. Make sure and keep this jacket as if it were yours, but always have it available for her. This will take you a long way with the girl you are looking to impress.

Body hair is good in places, and bad in others. Arms, armpits, and legs are the only places that you can just let grow. Your chest, back, and bellies can definitely have hair, but not a lot. If you are one of those poor guys that always are mistaken as the wolf man, then get it waxed or trimmed. Do not shave these areas, because it will grow back thicker. Absolutely the most important and trickiest area is your facial and neck hair. Absolutely no neck hair is allowed, however, facial hair is allowed in a variety of ways. This all depends upon the girl you are trying to attract. For example, clean shaven faces and goatees will attract a conservative woman. Beards are outdated though, so be careful with this one; only grow a beard if she suggests it. Your sideburns are important, too; they should match the style of the rest of your facial hair. My last note on facial hair is to keep it neat and trimmed. Do not grow long and shaggy beards and side-burns. They are not cool and take you back to the seventies. And always trim your nose and ear hair, and then wipe them out with Q-tips. Use as many Q-tips as you need—This is very important!

Now, I know this should absolutely be standard procedure for you by now, but BRUSH YOUR TEETH! This should be done on an average of three times a day: Morning, evening, and anytime you go to see her! On that note, use floss and Listerine as well. Another classic question is, gum or mints? Get whichever she prefers, but always have them on you and in use.

Do you keep a pair of fingernail and toenail clippers handy? This is another must have. A lady never wants to be scratched by your fingernails, so keep them short and clean. The very same goes for toenails. That way when you take off your shoes or are wearing sandals they look very presentable. While we are talking about hands, you should apply lotion to your hands two to three times a week. The ladies love muscular hands, but they only like to be touched by smooth hands. I understand that this is a fine line, but gentlemen its one that you will have to walk. Always buy the non-scented lotion, don't ever buy the fruity stuff or people might think you are a little fruity yourself! There are other body parts that you should apply lotion to as well. These include: Your feet, face, and neck.

Jewelry should always be kept to a minimum. A necklace, ear ring, or ring are all fine, but I wouldn't wear them all together. Save that money to buy jewelry for her. I realize that I am saying to do a lot of things for her, but believe me; you have no idea how many things she is and will be doing for you.

The last subject that I would like to address is that of scent. This subject is extremely important! Women will fall for you or flee from you dependent upon this one. They will be forgiving and a little bit understanding with all the other criterias, but not scent. This consists of several components actually; The first component we will address is the soap and shampoo that you use. You need to have soap with a more masculine, but clean scent. I recommend Irish Spring; it has a good clean scent that will not conflict with your cologne. Do not buy the fruity shampoos, in fact if you own any, throw them in the trash now, and go buy a different one! Women are not interested in cuddling up with a guy that smells like a girl. If you are not sure which one to buy, you can always ask your hairstylist. They will know which one will be good for you and your hair.

The next component is the lotion, aftershave, and deodorant that you use. Lotion should be a simple lotion with as little scent as you can find. Please don't waste your time looking for the most hydrating, smoothest, etc... lotion. Find one that works well and spend your time and efforts in other areas. The ladies will be ecstatic just knowing that you use lotion! The only areas you should put lotion on are your hands, face, neck, knees, elbows, and feet. Do this at least once every few days, but preferably everyday. I apply it immediately after I shave all those areas, with the exception of my feet. I put lotion on them right before I go to sleep for the night. Your aftershave should compliment your cologne; in fact, get the same scent if you can. Apply just enough to rub a little on your face and neck. Deodorant is also a very important component of your scent. You should find one that keeps you dry, as well as, mask any odor that you may develop. Once you find one that does this, find one with a slightly sweet, masculine scent. I prefer the spray-on because it is easier to apply and usually does not rub off on your clothes like the roll-ons do. However, a roll-on will work just fine, if you wait until you have your shirt on to apply it. I do the spray because I have forgotten so many times to wait to put it on until I have my shirt on. It gets kind of frustrating to look down and see white stripes on the bottoms of your shirts! You should also carry a spare deodorant in your vehicle for the unexpected event that you need it. And this will happen, so be prepared and have it on hand.

Take excellent care of your feet. Your feet can be a definite detriment to your overall scent. If you have stinky feet, buy foot odor products. There are tons of wonderful products on the market that will solve this problem for you. Also, make sure that your shoes do not stink. Once again, there are wonderful products on the market to cover you in this.

While on the subject of scent, we need to address your breath. You need to make sure that you remember to always have breath-fresheners handy. Remember, you can use gum or mints, or both, it doesn't matter—just use them!

The last component is the most important: your cologne! You should spend a good amount of time looking for the right one. Don't waste all your time looking for all the other components. Spend your time here! Do not, and I will reiterate DO NOT buy cheap cologne! You will smell like it, and women know exactly what it smells like. You don't want to smell cheap. That doesn't mean that the most expensive is the right choice either. This is a tough one! Once again I recommend taking a trusted female companion with you on this assignment. You need cologne that smells good on you to women—not only to you! You need to be careful with the sweet scents; I recommend sticking with the slightly musky scents or the clean scents. Girls are very particular about this. A lady can actually find an unattractive guy appealing if he is wearing really good cologne. So I leave this last thought with you on scent—IT WILL MAKE OR BREAK YOU!

Grooming is very important because girls relate their grooming to how they view themselves and they think guys do the same. They also want a guy that is confident, not arrogant, but yes, confident. Proper grooming will give you this appearance, which will open the door for you. So I will give you one last point on grooming—do it at home! Mirrors were not put in public for you to observe yourself, they were put there for the ladies. They do not want to see you constantly looking at yourself in the mirror. If you follow these rules you will be surprised how easy it will be to meet lovely ladies. However, these rules are not fool-proof, that is why the book continues on.

CHAPTER 2

Etiquette

Etiquette is very important. This is what will keep them around after you grab their attention with your great grooming habits. Just a forewarning on this subject, the rules do differ from location to location, as well as, woman to woman. However, I am going to try and give you the basics that will stay the same for the most part.

#1—Watch your language. Present your speech as if you are a prince, because you are! You are a child of the King! Act like it. Say beautiful things, joke, laugh, and have clean fun! I will address this little later on in the book. For now, be a man of few, but valuable words.

#2—Do not look at other women! This is next to impossible, but try your hardest. The reason I don't say, "Don't look at other women *when you are with her*" is that if you look when she is not around you are going to look when she is around. It is an extremely easy habit to form because they are "fearfully and wonderfully made"! I know that this is a tough one, but I make no apologies. If you want that special woman, then look at her like you do. She is worthy of your attention and should never lose that attention to

BE *Perfect* FOR HER

another woman! This is a Biblical principle. Let's read Matt 5:27-28 which says,

> Matt 5:27-28 "You have heard it said 'Do not commit adultery'. But I tell you that anyone who *looks* at a woman lustfully has already committed adultery with her in his heart." (NIV)

This means **don't look!** This will win you so many brownie points!

#3—The Bible calls them the weaker gender, treat them like they are!

> 1 Peter 3:7 "Husbands, in the same way be considerate as you live with your wives, and treat them with respect as the weaker partner and as heirs with you of the gracious gift of life, so that nothing will hinder your prayers."(NIV)

This means that you are to open the door, give her your hand when she stands, sits, and goes up and down stairs. It also means that you are to walk between her and any potential danger, such as the street, wildlife (snakes, bugs, dogs, etc...) and violent people. Use common sense with this one. If she doesn't want you to do these things for her, she will let you know. She will either tell you or do it herself. When I say to treat them as they are the weaker gender, I DO NOT mean that they are the inferior gender. There is no inferior gender! We both have our strengths and weaknesses. They are not as physically strong as we are, but they are strong! Imagine carrying a 8 pound sack of meat around with you, protruding from your body for 9 months and then having that 8 pounds of meat come out of your more delicate areas! Enough said. Treat them like they are your glory—The Bible says that they are.

#4—Give them the preference. This means that unless you are surprising them with a special restaurant, they get to decide where the two of you are going to eat. The only time you can budge on this is with a suggestion or if they don't have a preference. This also applies to your clothes, what activities the two of you do, how you do it, and when you do it! It does not apply to why you do it, SHE IS WHY YOU DO IT!

#5—Give her pleasant surprises. Flowers, candy, jewelry, cards, stuffed animals, her favorite romantic comedies, etc... Whatever good thing you can think of. You need to do this a minimum of once a month, if not every other week. Clothes of any sort are out. This will change should you be blessed enough to marry her! This principle should continue throughout the life of the relationship.

#6—Give her space. She needs to spend quality time with family and friends and so do you! This one is a fine line to walk though, because there is no set amount of time. You need to let her know that you want to be with her all the time, but you don't want her to forsake her family and friends.

#7—Compliment her often. Make sure your compliments are genuine and heart-felt, because women will see past any phony compliments. Tell her she is beautiful. Tell her how fabulous that dress looks on her! Don't compliment her too much, though. The times to compliment are pretty obvious: When you first see her, when you leave, when she changes clothes, when she feels ugly or down, in front of her friends and family, and when you are in that special moment when the two of you are staring in to each others eyes! You will learn to treasure those moments.

#8—Dress, eat, and drink your beverages neatly. If the lady you are with wanted a slob, she would be one herself! Would you find it attractive if she slurped her food, or let some of it fall back out of her mouth on the plate. If you have problems with things like this, follow two simple rules. Make sure your food is about 1/3 of what you can fit into your mouth before it ever leaves the plate, in other words, cut it neatly on the plate. The other rule is: Take your time eating. You are not at a race track—Slow down. By doing this your date with her might actually last longer. If you can do these two things, you will be in better shape than most guys out there.

#9—Always be willing to sacrifice your desires for her. This means go to the ballet, without degrading it. Watch a "chic-flic" with her. Go shopping with her. I don't mean to say do everything with her, you do need to have time for yourself and do things you enjoy. However, sacrifice these things for her some of the time and she will think the world of you, because if you make her the queen of your life, she will definitely make you the king!

Paul gave the charge for husbands to love their wives as Christ loved the church.

> Ephesians 5:25 "Husbands love your wives, just as Christ loved the church and gave himself up for her."(NIV)

Remember, "the church" is not a building, we as Christians are "the church". What a statement! Do you realize how much He loves us? Once again, what a statement! There are so many facets to this statement; however, I would like to focus on just one for now. If you can master this one the other ones will fall into place. Jesus said in Matt 20:28,

> Matthew 20:28 "just as the Son of Man did not come to be served, but to serve, and to give his life as a ransom for many."(NIV)

Gentlemen this is the key! If you will serve her and give your life as a ransom for her in all you do, most of these rules will just fall into place.

I do realize that the scripture says *husbands love your wives,* and you may not be there yet. However, if you will treat her like the gem of your life—she will be! So start practicing these rules now so God willing, she will be your wife someday!

CHAPTER 3

Communication

Communication is the relationship. This is the foundation, structure, roof, and everything that fills the house. This is the single most important thing in any relationship, because it is the substance of the relationship! Therefore I am going to spend, rather, invest time into this topic.

Communication on its most basic level is acknowledgement. Hello. Goodbye. How are you? How's life? These are all phrases we use to involve ourselves into someone else's life. They are just a few simple words that can move the mountains in people's lives. For example, if someone says, "hello", they have not only acknowledged your existence, but also the importance of your presence to them. They wouldn't have spoken to you if they didn't value, to some extent, your presence to them. Therefore, they give meaning to your presence, as far as they are concerned. How many times have you seen a beautiful woman who just walked by and didn't even say hello. Or even better—she says hello! What happens to you on the inside when either one of these scenarios happen? You will either feel unnoticed, neglected, undesirable, or important, valued, and desired. Why is this? Because she has just told you how important you are to her.

This is important, because we all have an internal desire to feel wanted by others in society.

Have you ever noticed how much women talk? They talk abundantly to almost anybody willing to listen to them, unless they already have an abundant source of listeners, hence the snobs—they already have their desired listeners. This denotes that people have a hierarchy of communication. They have their elect and their commoners.

We all like to feel we are the elect in a conversation. Which is why you feel important when that beautiful woman walks by and says "hi"; she is giving meaning to your presence, and you feel somewhat important to her.

Women feel similar emotions, even more so than we do. They have such a strong desire to feel wanted and noticed, and for someone to think they are beautiful. This is your job, rather, your mission in the relationship. If you can find a way to make her feel wanted, desirable, valuable, beautiful, and important, you will not have any problem getting her to talk with you. However, if she feels insecure in any of these feelings—she will bottle up and not talk with you. So you need to communicate to her that she is valuable, desirable, beautiful, and important to you. You can do some of this by talking to her. But the best way is by your non-verbal communication. Are you listening, smiling, holding her hand, standing up when she walks into the room, and opening doors for her? These are the absolute best ways to communicate to her how you feel about her. How are you standing? Are you yawning or looking out into the distance and interrupting her to tell her about your opinions and experiences. That's horrible! You have just told her that what she has to say is not important enough for you to give your attention to. And on top of that you have just made her feel insecure about herself and what she has to say. An important point to remember is women are **ALWAYS** looking for security.

The same principle works when you are talking with a woman. You want her full attention, this is one way that she can make you feel important, valued, and desired. The power of life and death are in the tongue,

> Proverbs 18:21 "The tongue has the power of life and death, those who love it will eat its fruit."(NIV)

You absolutely need to be able to carry on a conversation with them. If you cannot talk to them and make them feel valued they will not be interested in you!

You need to practice being an excellent listener. Women need to express themselves frequently, and they do it the most often through speech. She needs to express her thoughts, emotions, and ideas to you. Therefore, you need to listen—intently, because she will tell you everything you need to know! Through this medium, she will tell you how to win her heart and how to make her happy. She will tell you what she thinks of you, God, and life directly through her speech. She does this by just talking about whatever is on her mind. This will also tell you what she thinks about the most. And those are the topics you should learn and talk to her the most about. Communication is a powerful tool, in which, you can use to build other people up. People need to talk; especially females and they need to know that they are being heard. Therefore you have the opportunity to build her faith by listening to her and encouraging her! However, keep it very practical and DO NOT be insistent and repetitious, this is very unattractive coming from either party.

A very critical thought to remember is women are just as smart as you are, however they do not think like you think. They not only understand fashion, kids, food, and other stereotypical areas, but they also understand business, politics, and yes—some ladies even understand sports! So when you are talking to them, talk about subjects they bring up often. If you do not know these subjects, learn them by listening to her. You have no idea how much this will impress her. Think about it, she will try to understand things you do and talk about, so you should do the same for her! But whatever you do, do not limit her to the traditional things women do. We do not live in a traditional society and she is not a traditional woman. She is a virtuous woman and those traditional things do not bestow virtue on her. Her attitude, morals, and motives do!

The toughest part of this whole process is being able to interpret her language. This is where the communication lines have been cut. We (men) need to re-attach them to our brains, so we can do right by her. That is the main purpose for this book—to help you understand the way that she views things, so you can respond accordingly. The most amazing part of this whole process is that you can learn and understand her. This is very exciting news! It is also very simple. Pray, learn (pay attention), and do as James says,

> James 1:19 "Be quick to listen, slow to speak, and slow to anger!" (NIV)

Notice that in this verse it says to ONLY be quick to listen. Why do you suppose that this is? It is the same reason God spoke to Elijah through a still small voice. It is the same reason Jesus prayed that His disciples would have ears to hear. God wanted Elijah to be attentive and listen closely to His words. Jesus wanted his disciples to have understanding and wisdom, that comes by listening and discerning. Words are powerful they will tell you everything you need to know. God's word created you, me, and the heavens and earth, and His word will judge the heavens and the earth, as well as you and I!

> Romans 10:17 "Consequently, faith comes from hearing the message, and the message is heard through the word of Christ." (NIV)

Paul says that, faith comes by hearing, and hearing by the Word of God. In other words, it comes by hearing people speak God's Word. With this said, it is extremely imperative when you are dating, to talk about God, the Bible and how both of you view spiritual matters. Faith is the wanted result in this scripture, faith pleases God and it comes by HEARING THE WORD OF GOD! Speaking brings the word of faith out into the open. Therefore, gain faith by hearing and then you will be able to speak it. Because the Bible doesn't say to not speak, but to be slow about it. We are to be slow to speak and slow to anger. It goes on in James 1:20 to say that,

> James 1:20 "The anger of man does not accomplish the righteousness of God" (NIV)

But hearing does! This way you can speak wisely in light of the fact that we will be judged by our words. Jesus said in Matthew 12:36-37,

> Matthew 12:36-37 "But I tell you that men will have to give account on the Day of Judgment for every careless word they have spoken. For by your words you will be acquitted, and by your words you will be condemned."

That, my friends, is what we call a sobering scripture. You also will either be justified or condemned in the company of women by your words. So listen and be wise in your speech!

The first facet of speaking is the value of your words. Do you do what you say you will do? You are only as good as your word. This is an eternal principle, as well as, a measure of the man you are to her. Therefore, be slow to speak and you will save yourself a lot of heartache.

The second facet is the quality of the words you use. I honestly hope you are not using profanity, but I also hope you are not speaking vain words. This basically means empty words, which serve no purpose. You need to learn new words so you can ascertain to communicate on an advanced level with her and not look ignorant.

There are so many things to learn on communication, and this is literally the tip of the iceberg. I recommend foremost reading the Bible, taking classes at college, joining a club, like Toastmaster's, or reading books on communication, just like you are doing now! With that said: This is by no means a completed work on communication, but rather a launching point to help ensure that you are able to start and maintain a healthy relationship. So study up!

CHAPTER 4

Servant Hood

Servanthood is the key to having a successful career, social life, family life, marital life, and most importantly a godly life. Do you remember in the chapter 2, we talked about Jesus not coming to be served, but rather to serve. This definitely applies to your relationship with women. Jesus also said that the **greatest** among you shall be the **servant.**

> Mark 10:41-45 "When the ten heard about this, they became indignant with James and John. Jesus called them together and said 'you know that those who are regarded as rulers of the Gentiles lord it over them. And their high officials exercise authority over them. Not so with you. Instead, whoever wants to become great among you must be your servant, and whoever wants to be first must be slave of all.'" (NIV)

What a statement! Let's look at and examine a few characters in the Bible that really lived this statement out.

If you haven't read the story of Joseph in Genesis, you need to at this point in time to get an understanding of what we are about to discuss (Genesis 37-48). If you are familiar with it, please read on! He was sold into slavery and eventually became as the Pharaoh in Egypt. There is a lot more to his life than just this and that is exactly what we are looking for. Joseph was the second youngest of twelve brothers, but he was his father's favorite. Out of jealously and pride, Joseph's brothers sold him to the Midianites, who bought him as a slave. The Midianites then sold him to Potiphar as a servant. While in Potiphar's house he does such a great job with all that he is given, Potiphar eventually promotes him to controlling his entire household, with the exception of Potiphar's wife. Can you imagine your boss promoting you to the point where you control even his personal finances? That is exactly what happened here. Potiphar's wife then tried to seduce Joseph day after day, but he refused to give in to her.

Why was Joseph promoted to the highest position in Potiphar's household? What did he do that was so different from the rest of Potiphar's servants? I believe the answer is found in Joseph's response to Potiphar's wife when she wanted to sleep with him. This passage is found in Gen 39:9,

> Genesis 39:9 "No one in this house is greater than I am. My master has withheld nothing from me except you because you are his wife. How then could I do such a wicked thing and sin against God?" (NIV)

Joseph says, how can I commit this sin against God? Joseph does mention Potiphar in this passage, but his main focus is on God. Why? Joseph was serving Potiphar, but more importantly he was serving God. That is true servanthood, doing everything as unto the Lord.

God gave Joseph dreams during his youth, and Joseph knew that he needed to serve God in everything, for them to be fulfilled. Paul actually addresses this in Eph 6:5-8, by telling slaves to obey their masters as unto the Lord.

> Ephesians 6:5-8 "Slaves, obey your earthly masters with respect and fear, and with sincerity of heart, just as you would obey Christ. Obey them not only to win their favor when their eye is on you, but like slaves of Christ, doing the will of God from your heart. Serve wholeheartedly, as if you were serving the Lord, not men, because you know that the Lord will reward everyone for whatever good he does, whether he is slave or free." (NIV)

I believe the key to being a great servant for God is being a great servant for God in whatever position He has you in life. It is not about what position you hold in life, it is about what you do with it, what kind of attitude you approach it with, and where your heart and motives are.

The key characteristics of Joseph being a great servant were in the words that he spoke when he was confronted with sinning against his earthly master. Jesus said that out of the abundance in your heart, your mouth will speak.

> Luke 6:45 "The good man brings good things out of the good stored up in his heart, and the evil man brings evil things out of the evil stored up in his heart. For out of the overflow of his heart his mouth speaks." (NIV)

This means that when you have to make an immediate response to something—what comes out of your mouth tells everyone where your heart is. In other terms, when you accidentally hit your finger with a hammer, stub your toe, or you are caught in a stressful situation, what comes out of your mouth? Is it swear words, lies, deceit, or the truth, God's word, and blessings. That tells everyone where your heart is. The state of your heart dictates your words. Joseph's heart response was, how then could I do such a wicked thing and sin against God? What would you have done?

The key to having a right heart is doing the right thing Biblically speaking with the right attitude day after day, year after year—consistently. This is why it is pertinent to read and study God's word, so you will know God's Law and what He expects from you. And did you ever wonder why David called our God a Rock. God is faithful, even when we are unfaithful. Gentlemen its time we take after our heavenly Father and be a rock in goodness and moral integrity!

The story of Joseph does not end here; God gave Joseph dreams throughout his youth, and as a result Joseph knew that he needed to serve God in everything, for his dreams to be fulfilled. By being faithful to God with the heart of a servant, he eventually makes it all the way to the highest possible position in Egypt, with the exception of being a Pharaoh. Joseph's brothers had sold him into slavery, but by being a great servant he became the second most powerful man in Egypt. However, the most amazing part of Joseph's story is the way he treats his brothers when he has all the earthly power to get even with them. The whole region is going through a crippling famine, Joseph's brothers come to him, being second to the Pharoah, and ask him for food for their families. This is the greatest part of the story of Joseph, not only his resistance to Potiphar's wife, but choosing to forgive and serve his brothers. What? He could have wiped them off the face of the Earth! Instead he chose to serve God, by serving those who would have been his enemies. Why would anyone in their right mind ever serve those who sought to kill him! Hmmm... Does this remind you of Jesus? In the Garden of Gethsemane soldiers came to arrest Jesus, so Peter, defending Jesus, cut the ear off of the servant of the high priest. Then Jesus turned to Peter and told him,

> Matthew 26:52-53 "Put your sword back in its place... Do you think I cannot call on my Father, and he will at once put at my disposal more than twelve legions of angels?" (NIV)

Jesus, so full of love and forgiveness, turns and heals the servant and goes with the mob. Jesus is saying, I can rescue myself, but I will go with the soldiers, because it God's will. Later while hanging on the cross, he asked forgiveness for those who put Him there. **HAVE YOU EVER STOPPED TO THINK THAT THIS LIFE IS NOT ALL ABOUT YOU?!!!**

It's not about you, **IT IS ABOUT GOD!** Jesus set the example for us that many other servants of God have also set for us. It is about **Him**—winning people to **Him,** loving on people for **Him,** giving your all to and for **Him. It is about living out His will for your life.** It is about **Him.** The sooner you come to this conclusion the better off you will be. John the Baptist said this in John 3:30,

> John 3:30 "He must become greater; I must become less."(NIV)

There were never truer words spoken from a true servant of God. A good servant must put their Master's orders, needs, and desires above their own. Even Jesus did this. In Phil 2:1-8, it talks about having the same attitude that Jesus had, by taking the nature of a bondservant.

> Philippians 2:1-8 "If you have any encouragement from being united with Christ, if any comfort from his love, if any fellowship with the Spirit, if any tenderness and compassion, then make my joy complete by being like-minded, having the same love, being one in spirit and purpose. Do nothing out of selfish ambition or vain

conceit, but in humility consider others better than yourselves. Each of you should look not only to your own interests, but also to the interest of others. Your attitude should be the same as Christ Jesus. Who, being the same nature God, did not consider equality with God something to be grasped, but made himself nothing taking the very nature of a servant, being made in human likeness. And being found in appearance as a man, he humbled himself and became obedient to death – even death on a cross." (NIV)

There is a huge difference between a servant (slave) and a bond-servant. A bondservant is one who has already "done his time", so to speak, and has *chosen* to stay behind and continue serving his master. Jesus did not have to die on the cross for us—He *chose* to die on the cross for us! In this same manner, you should choose to serve one another and most importantly your Heavenly Master!

My goal in life is for God to call me His friend. I honestly believe that we should all have goals in our relationship with God. If you think about it, how many people in scripture are known as friends of God? Not many. Why do you suppose that is so? I think it is because of the nature of friendship. It requires giving intimate knowledge of yourself to another and having absolute trust in that other person to value and protect that knowledge. I believe we can all call Jesus our friend, but how many of you can Jesus call His friend? Can you be trusted with His most intimate secrets? That is why it is so important for me to have God call me His friend. I want that closeness with God. Let's look at scripture to see how we can achieve that closeness.

Paul talks about this when he says,

Philippians 3:14 "I press on toward the mark of the prize of the high calling of God in Christ Jesus." (KJV)

What is the High Calling of God in Christ Jesus? I believe this statement is one that we can find in the life of Jesus; because it says "in Christ Jesus", so we should be able to see it in His life. In Matt 20:26 it talks about the chief of you shall be the servant of all.

Matthew 20:26 "Not so with you. Instead, whoever wants to become great among you must be your servant," (NIV)

So if the chief, or we can say "Highest Called Officer", is the servant of all, then Jesus' "Highest Calling" was to be the servant of all. Hence, Paul being in tune with the Holy Spirit, knew that the "Highest Calling" was to be the servant of all. Therefore, Phil 3:14 would read, "I press toward the mark of the prize of the *servanthood of God to all* in Christ Jesus" (Words in italics mine). I hope this gives you a little more light on this verse. Now, let's dig even deeper into this passage. What is the "mark of the prize"? Let's start with the word "mark". This is a fairly simple term to decipher; it is tied to the word marksmanship. In other words, someone who is an expert at aiming and hitting the center of a target is a good marksman, or a good shot.

What Paul is talking about here is the center of the target, and that is the "mark". So Paul wants to win the prize by aiming at being a servant of God to all in Christ Jesus.

What is the "prize" then? We all know what the term "prize" means. It means a treasure that a person wins by being the best at something. So, what is the treasure here? I believe the treasure here is to be a friend of God. What a treasure—to have the Creator of the Universe disclose His deepest thoughts and plans to you. Very few people in the Bible actually had this relationship with God. There are very few people who God called His friend, which I recall: Enoch,

Abraham, Moses, and the Apostles. I might have missed a few, but the point is this: How many people did God use in the Bible? Thousands. How many people are listed here—15. What does that tell you about friendship with God?

How I came to the conclusion that the "prize" is friendship with God, is by what I found Jesus saying to some of His disciples. In John 15:15,

> John 15:15 "I no longer call you servants, because a servant does not know his master's business. Instead, I have called you friends, for everything that I learned from my Father I have made known to you." (NIV)

You can "no longer be called a servant" if you were never called a servant. In other words, what qualified them to become "no longer a servant" was the fact that they had already been His servants. However, do you notice the progression to friendship that Jesus teaches His disciples here? Firstly, they become a servant, secondly, they learn the master's business, and at the appropriate time by proving themselves, they become friends by learning what the Father had made known to Jesus. Therefore, to complete our paraphrase of Phil 3:14 *"I aim toward the center of the target, which is Jesus calling me his friend, by becoming the servant of God to all in Christ Jesus."* (words in italics mine). Does this make more sense to you? It does to me. I need to serve others just like I would serve Jesus, so I can someday be called His friend.

Before I finish this chapter, which many books could be written on, I want to complete talking about John 15, because this is such a rich chapter. There is one other thing that qualifies you for friendship with Christ, and it is found in verse 14. It states,

John 15:14 "You are my friends if you do what I command." (NIV)

If you will read John 15:9-17 it will give you the whole context.

John 15:9-17 "As the Father has loved me, so have I loved you. Now remain in my love. If you obey my commands, you will remain in my love, just as I have obeyed my Father's commands and remain in his love. I have told you this so that my joy may be in you and that your joy may be complete. My command is this: Love each other as I have loved you. Greater love has no one than this, that he lay down his life for his friends. You are my friends if you do what I command. I no longer call you servants, because a servant does not know his master's business. Instead, I have called you friends, for everything that I learned from my Father I have made known to you. You did not choose me, but I chose you and appointed you to go and bear fruit – fruit that will last. Then the Father will give you whatever you ask in my name. This is my command: Love each other." (NIV)

The key to being a great disciple, servant, and precious friend of Jesus is by loving each other. He only gave us two commands, period. They are found in Matt 22:36-40.

Matthew 22:36-40 ""Teacher, which is the greatest commandment in the Law?" Jesus replied "Love the Lord your God with all your heart and with all your soul and with all your mind. This is the first and greatest commandment. And the second is like it: Love your neighbor as yourself. All the Law and Prophets hang on these two commandments." (NIV)

Have you opened your Bible and read these scriptures for yourself yet? These are two verses in the Bible that you **need to know** and have memorized. Jesus said that "The Law and the Prophets hang on these two commandments." That is quite a statement! The Law and

The Prophets are the whole Old Testament! He said that these books hang on the two commandments. He did not say that they are derived from or supported by, or the foundation for the Law and The Prophets—He said that The Law and the Prophets would not exist without these two commands. The Law and the Prophets (the whole Old Testament) are absolutely dependent on them and there would be **no** Old Testament without them. So why should you study the Old Testament, if you don't even understand what keeps it in the picture? That is why the next chapter is on… you guessed it—Love.

CHAPTER 5

Love defined

This is the most revolutionary chapter of the whole book! Not only are we going to change the way you look at this subject, we are also going to change the way that you approach it. Let me start out with one of the biggest misunderstandings. The word "love" does not mean the same in the English language as it does in other languages. For example "I love this burrito!" and "I love my wife!" carry an absolutely different context to them, yet we use the same word for both statements. Our love of food is not comparable to the love towards our life mate. We are not physically, mentally, or emotionally able to love a burrito. And YES—I did use the words *life* mate, because Jesus *never* endorsed divorce. In Mark 10:4-9

Mark 10:4-9 "They said "Moses permitted a man to write a certificate of divorce and send her away." "It was because your hearts were hard that Moses wrote you this law," Jesus replied. "But at the beginning of creation God made them male and female. For this reason a man will leave his father and mother and be united to his wife, and the two will become one flesh. So they are no longer two, but one. Therefore what God has joined together, let man not separate." (NIV)

Jesus stated that it was because of the hardness of peoples hearts that Moses permitted divorce as a result of unfaithfulness, but it was not so in the beginning… "therefore what God has joined together, let man not separate." In light of this, your wife will be your "life mate".

The word love is greatly misunderstood in the English language. In fact, the devil has capitalized on the misunderstanding of this word. That is, after all, what he does. The devil's goal is to cause confusion and disorder. Think about this—What is the number one thing humanity writes songs about? That's right—Love. What is listed as the greatest virtue in the Bible (1 Cor. 13:13)?

> 1 Corinthians 13:13 "And now these three remain: faith, hope and love. But the greatest of these is love." (NIV)

Once again—Love. And what do you think Satan's greatest deception is? Hmmm…—Love? Absolutely! We live in a society that is constantly pounded with different meanings of love compacted into one word. What a huge mistake! Is it any wonder why people don't believe God loves them? Taking into consideration they don't understand what "God loves you" even means. So let's use a different language to describe the different types of love. I personally believe the Greek language has the best variety of words and definitions for this particular word.

1. Eros

The first Greek word for love that I will elaborate on is the word "eros". This word is always used in reference to sexual affection. In other words, most of the songs that you here on the radio saying I Love You, are saying I want to have sex with you. This is not the love that you want to base your relationship on. Fornication is one of the few sins listed in the Bible that will not allow you to enter into kingdom of God (Gal 5:19-21).

> Galatians 5:19-21 "The acts of the sinful nature are obvious: sexual immorality, impurity and debauchery; idolatry and witchcraft; hatred, discord, jealousy, fits of rage, selfish ambition, dissensions, factions and envy; drunkenness, orgies, and the like. I warn you, as I did before, that those who live like this will not inherit the kingdom of God."(NIV)

It will be impossible to have a holy dating relationship if you are basing your relationship on "eros". If you are in a relationship like this, repent (stop sinning) and ask God for forgiveness.

2. Phileo

The next most common word for love is "phileo". This one should be easy to remember—just think about the city of brotherly love "____delphia". So, the definition of "phileo" is brotherly love. There you go! There are three others I am going to mention in passing, just for reference's sake. They are: "philaguria"—the love of money, "philautos"—the love of self, and "philostorgos"—the love of relatives. There are several others, but my hope is to give you knowledge on how to "love" women. Therefore there is one other I am going to mention, and it is the one we are going to dwell on.

3. Agape

Agape is the most important word in the New Testament. Agape love is the God kind of love. Jesus gave us only two commandments and they both consist of this word.

> Matthew 22:36-40 ""Teacher, which is the greatest commandment in the Law?" Jesus replied "Love the Lord your God with all your

heart and will all your soul and with all your mind. This is the first and greatest commandment. And the second is like it: Love your neighbor as yourself. All the Law and Prophets hang on these two commandments." (NIV)

Paul also said, "The greatest of these is love".

1 Corinthians 13:13 "And now these three remain: faith, hope and love. But the greatest of these is love." (NIV)

And John said God is Love.

1 John 4:16 "And so we know and rely on the love God has for us. God is love. Whoever lives in love lives in God, and God in him." (NIV)

What an important word! Yet we don't have a precise definition of what it truly means. "Love can be known only from the actions it prompts." is what Vine's Complete Expository Dictionary of the Old and New Testament Words says. So if this is the case we can define the meaning of the word agape using this statement. The Holy Spirit showed me that when Jesus was in the Garden of Gethsemane (Matt 26:36-39),

Matthew 26:36-39 "Then Jesus went with his disciples to a place called Gethsemane, and he said to them 'Sit here while I go over there and pray.' He took Peter and the two sons of Zebedee along with him, and he began to be sorrowful and troubled. Then he said to them 'My soul is overwhelmed with sorrow to the point of death. Stay here and keep watch with me' Going a little farther, he fell with his face to the ground and prayed, 'My Father, if it is possible, may this cup be taken from me. Yet not as I will, but as you will.'" (NIV)

He gave us the greatest display of agape love. Jesus knew he would be crucified, He asked the Father if this cup could pass from Him. His emotions were crying out, asking if there was any way to stop what was about to happen. His next words say it all, "Not My will be done, but Yours". What an amazing statement! This tells me several major things about agape love. First of all, it is not based on emotion, but rather commitment. This should change a lot of perceptions of what the "God kind of love" truly means. Jesus' emotions were saying, STOP! But something deeper rose up from within Him, saying I am committed, dedicated, and willing to do what the Father would have me to do—even the most horrific, agonizing death. Once again—What a statement! It was a choice. He said, "I don't want to do this," and He could have called a legion of angels to rescue Him if He so chose.

> Matthew 26:53 " Do you think I cannot call on my Father, and he will at once put at my disposal more than twelve legions of angels?" (NIV)

But that is what is so profound about His love for the Father and us—He chose not to. This is what motivated me to come to salvation. I didn't understand all the dynamics of it at the time, but I understood that Jesus died so that I could be saved from my sin. He loves me. That sparked love in me for Him and it grows constantly in the sight of His lovingkindness. He is so good to me, I can't help but grow in love and respect for Him.

So let's recap with the best definition we have, from this viewpoint. Agape is a choice of commitment and dedication, not based on emotions, but stemming from a desire to perform the Father's good will in a life or situation. WOW! This is not the fullness of this word or its meaning, however it is an attempt I believe God will bless us in our understanding and knowledge of this word. Based on this definition of the word, our understanding of many verses should change in the Bible. With this definition one could say, the Lord Jesus chooses to commit and dedicate Himself to me, not based on emotions, but rather stemming from a desire to perform the Father's good will in my life. In Matt 22:36-40

> Matthew 22:36-40 ""Teacher, which is the greatest commandment in the Law?" Jesus replied "Love the Lord your God with all your heart and will all your soul and with all your mind. This is the first and greatest commandment. And the second is like it: Love your neighbor as yourself. All the Law and Prophets hang on these two commandments." (NIV)

The first commandment is to "love the Lord God with all your heart, with all your soul, with all your mind" the second commandment, Jesus said, is "to love your neighbor as you love yourself". According to our definition of agape, it should read: Commit and dedicate yourself to your neighbor, not based on how you feel towards them, but rather stemming from a desire to see God's good will in their lives, as you have the same desire to see God's good will in your life. That totally changed my perception of how to treat my neighbor (which really means anyone that God brings you in contact with). That is why you will often hear certain ministers instructing you to not be ruled by your emotions. If you are ruled by your emotions, you will not be loving people the way the Bible leads us to. Joyce Meyer has some excellent material on this.

Another extremely important aspect of the second commandment is a statement that Jesus made. He said, "The second commandment is like unto the first"(Matt 22:39). This means it is not the same, but just as important as the first commandment. I asked God why this was and He answered me with Matthew 25:40

> Matthew 25:40 "The King will reply 'I tell you the truth, whatever you did for one of the least of these brothers of mine, you did for me.'" (NIV)

This means that by loving our neighbor we are loving Him. This explains why loving our neighbor is just as important as loving Him! But I still wanted more understanding, so I asked Him why loving my neighbor was loving Him. This time He answered me out of one of my favorite books in the Bible, 1 John 4:20-21

> 1 John 4:20-21 "if anyone says "I love God," yet hates his brother, he is a liar. For anyone who does not love his brother, whom he has seen, cannot love God, whom he has not seen. And he has given us this command: Whoever loves God must also love his brother." (NIV)

The key statement in verse 20 is that if a man cannot love his brother he has seen, how can he love God whom he hasn't seen? The answer is if we cannot love the only "image of God" (our brother) we have, then how can we love God? He gave us an image of himself to love, if we cannot love that image, then how can you love God, whom you haven't seen?

Therefore, choose to dedicate yourself to your neighbor, regardless of how you feel towards them, and desire to see God's Good will in their lives, because they are the image of God! I most importantly choose to commit and dedicate myself, regardless of my emotions, to my Father, because I desire to see His desires fulfilled.

With this new foundation and understanding of love, we will proceed to how it is properly used in a relationship. There are times when more than one of the "loves" are used, in fact it seems that more often than not, more than one meaning of "love" is used. For example, someone who is friends with their parents, not only uses "philostorgos" (respectful love of relatives), but also "phileo" (friendly, brotherly type of love), and "agape", because obviously they desire to see God's good will in their lives. I could give example after example, but I hope by now that you get the point.

In a marriage relationship, there should be four types of love: agape, eros, phileo, and philostorgos. All of these seem obvious, however, there needs to be a hierarchy structure set up on which love should have the precedence. Here it is: agape, phileo, philostorgos, and last and least eros. The reason for this order is to keep the relationship the way God designed it to be.

The reason that eros is last is simple—if left unchecked, it can dominate and decimate a relationship. It is the only one of the loves that has a direct tie to our flesh, therefore, it is also the easiest to corrupt. In fact, our culture alone testifies to this. We live in a culture that is saturated with sin and laden down with sexual immorality. It sickens me to see something so sacred taken and made twisted, uncontrollable, and a lure, especially for young men, bringing them into bondage that can utterly ruin their life. I hate pornography for so many reasons, it is a sin against God and poisons your view of women, God's most beautiful creation. Satan uses this to try to turn any woman that walks by into an object of sexual desire for you. God did not and does not EVER intend a woman to be viewed in this way. There should be only one woman your attention is drawn to and it should be for so many other reasons than this one. Stay as far as you can away from sexual sins—it will only do you and your future wife harm. I beg you to leave this area of society alone. It will take everything you have and leave you with nothing. There is a good reason Paul singles these particular sins out in,

1 Corinthians 6:18 "Flee from sexual immorality. All sins a man commits are outside his body, but he who sins sexually sins against his own body." (NIV)

This chapter could have been turned into a very long series of encyclopedias, but I chose to make a few points in it to spurn you on. I want to help build a foundation in your life with these teachings, with a fervent hope that you will seek God for the rest of your life!

CHAPTER 6

Family and Friends

Gentlemen, this one is a hard one to talk about. There are so many societal rules on this subject and I am still learning them myself. You need to spend time with her and you need to spend time with her family, and she needs to spend time with your family. With that said, the most important of the three is the time you spend with her.

The Parents—this is not as challenging as what you would think. Just be a servant and always be respectful. Always open the door for them, and be the first one to offer to help do anything that they might need done, with the exception, that their request is beyond your scope of expertise. For example, do not offer to overhaul their engine, unless you are an auto mechanic and so on. The most important thing that you can do is to show them how great of a leader and example you will be for their daughter in righteousness. Let's digest this word for a minute so it actually has some relevance to our conversation. Righteousness in its simplest terms means a state of being that is found to be right. Or in other words, if you are righteous, you are being what God created you to be.

Creation is a great way to get a good understanding of what righteousness means. Let's say that you are an ingenious robotics technician and you design a great robot. What characteristics would you like it to have? Why? Really, take this thought and run with it. Sit this book down now and think about what characteristics you would want your robot to have. What if your robot does the opposite of what you intended? What state of being would the robot be in? A wrong one of course! That is the definition of unrighteousness. It isn't doing what it is supposed to do. Let's say that it performs everything to a "t" that you want it to. What would your creation be considered? Right, it would be in a state of being right. That is called righteousness. That is what Jesus was, He was God's creation like us, but lived his life and made decisions the way God intended him to. He was righteous. Guess what! You are the righteousness of God through Christ Jesus; you received that by believing in Him. The challenge is living it every day by renewing your mind with His word. Jesus did it and He is our strength, so we can do it. Therefore, be righteous in front of her parents. This will win you their favor as well as hers!

Do you remember the chapter on communication? It is very effective for parents, too. James 1:21 says,

James 1:19 "Be quick to listen, slow to speak, and slow to anger!" (NIV)

Wow, if you can do this in front of her parents… They will think you are the most mature guy that they have ever met! So don't be overly talkative, but answer and carry on a conversation when spoken to. Let them do the majority of the talking. They are the ones interviewing you for suitability of their daughter. Be a man of few, but powerful words and you will knock their socks off!

Impressing her brothers and sisters will involve a lot more of playing it by ear, although, you do need to do this with the parents as well. Let her tell you what she wants your relationship with her family to be. If you will just be polite and respectful to her siblings—that usually will make her happy and it will gain their respect. Be talkative, but once again, be a man of few, but powerful words!

Getting to know her friends, believe it or not, will more than likely be your biggest challenge. They can make your relationship easy or difficult. Do not involve your guy friends with her unless absolutely necessary! She did not date you for your guy friends and you did not date her for her girlfriends. If a friendship is supposed to happen here, then it will happen over a period of time without a forced effort, and she will do most of the instigating. Once you are a more mature couple, you will start to develop friendships with other couples and you will really enjoy those.

Keep your relationship simple! The more people that you involve into your relationship issues, the more complicated it will get. I definitely recommend keeping your dating relationship just between the two of you and both of your parents. There are only a few exceptions to this rule, one of them is if God brings experienced and mature people into your lives that you know are led to give you advice.

I know that this is a short chapter, but if you will build this on top of the other foundations that we have already laid in the other chapters—you will be fine. Family and friends can have adverse effects on your relationship, if you don't know their place in your relationship. However, if you do—they can be one of the biggest blessings to your relationship. Prayer is always the best answer and the most comprehensive one that I will offer to you. If you will ask God for wisdom and guidance, He will give it. We know that it is

His will to lead and guide us, because He sent the Holy Spirit for this purpose.

CHAPTER 7

God

Your relationship with God is the most important relationship that you will ever have. Have you ever wondered what the meaning of life was? What were we created to do? It is very simple. If you will read the first three chapters of Genesis you will discover that the meaning of our life is to have a relationship with God. He didn't create us just to sit around so He can watch us for entertainment. He created us to love Him. If you do this, you will notice that everything else in life will be taken care of. If you will think about Him first thing in the morning, throughout the day, and then think of Him lastly before you go to sleep—you will see your Love for Him grow, and experience His love towards you.

But there is a lot more to your relationship with God than just thinking about Him. You have to thank Him. You have to tell others what He has done for you. When you pray to Him, thank Him for what He has done for you. Do you pray each day? If so—how often? And most importantly, what do your prayers consist of? These are pretty accurate indicators as to where your relationship is with God. Quite a reality check, Huh? Well, here is another: All of the rest of this book is pointless without this chapter. POINTLESS!!! The rest of the chapters in this book **hang** on this one! I hope you remember this reference from the Love defined chapter. The rest of this book would not exist without the content of this chapter; in fact, you and I would not exist without it!

So, where is your relationship at with Him? Do some praying and searching on this before you read any further...

Praying will move you closer to God, he wants you to know where you stand with him. Now, where do you want to go in your relationship with Him? Do you know where He wants you to go? Have you asked Him yet? Whether you have or have not—Let's do that together right now. Pray this prayer with me: Father, I know why you have created me. What do you want me to be? Show me how to go deeper into my relationship with You. You have revealed this to your servants this throughout the ages, now I come as a servant and as a son. I know that I have what I ask for according to 1 John 5:14-15. I also ask that you would show me the richness of Your love, and that I could show that love to others as well. Thank you for revealing Yourself to me—I Love you Father, I love you Jesus, I love you Holy Spirit. Thank you for guiding me into the greatest relationship I will ever know. Amen.

Now that we have asked Him, we must prepare for His answer. A lot of times He will reveal something to us to get us started. He is waiting to see if we are eagerly seeking Him, and He will progressively reveal the rest of it to us. Consistency is so important, that is what God is looking for in you. Your relationship with Him will progress throughout your whole life when you are consistently praying and patiently waiting on His answers. I have some helpful suggestions on how to hear from Him. Remember, this is a personal relationship with God—not a corporate. Sharing with other people what God has revealed to you is a great thing to do, God wants you to have fellowship with other Christians and share the wonderful things he has showed you. There should be some discernment in this as well, though. You don't have to go out and tell people everything that God tells you, some things are only between Him and you! With that said, are you an early riser in the morning? If not, it's time to change. That doesn't mean that you need to get up before 6:00 A.M. What it does mean, is that you need to wake up with enough time to pray and read your Bible. Do NOT read and pray while you are doing your other morning routines. Not to say that prayer can't carry over into them, but it deserves the highest priority! Your focus should be on God, remember the still small voice he spoke to Elijah with? He speaks to us with that still small voice as well, so if you are doing other things while praying and your focus isn't completely on God you are taking a chance of not hearing His voice or instruction. Remember in the chapter about communication: it is the roof, the foundation, and everything else in the house. The same applies with your prayer life.

I am not going to tell you how to pray, because there are thousands of books on the subject and the Bible is full of prayers, but what I am going to tell you to do—is to make it personal. Make it intimate. Reveal your heart to God and He will reveal His to you. Talk with Him like a Father, Friend, Master, Teacher, like He is your God—Because He is all these things and more. The more passionate you become about Him, the more passionately He will reveal Himself in your life. Be honest with Him and speak the Truth (His Word) about your self. Tell Him what His word says about Him.

The most important thing you can do is to use His name! If you haven't figured it out by now—I LOVE the book of Phillipians. Let's look at it again. Read Phil. 2:9-11.

Philippians 2:9-11 "Therefore God exalted him to the highest place and gave him the name that is above every name, that at the name of Jesus every knee should bow, in heaven and on earth and under the earth, and every tongue confess that Jesus Christ is Lord, to the glory of the Father." (NIV)

Did you notice what it said about the name of Jesus? It is the name above every name. What about the other names of God? Why would Jesus be above any other name of God? It is relatively simple if you think about it. I am sure by now that you have heard some of the different names of God and what they mean. If not, Lester Sumrall had a great book on this called "The Names of God", and you need to get it and read it! I am not going to go into a long narrative about what each of the names of God mean; rather the promises associated with them. For example, Jehovah Repheka had the promise of healing associated with it. Jehovah Shalom means the Lord is my peace, He is promising us peace. El Shaddai means that God is more than enough, God is promising us that he is everything we need. There are many other names of God and they were always associated with a covenant that had conditions that were required to be met before the promise could be claimed. One of the MANY wonderful things that Jesus the Christ did for us was fulfill these conditions for the promises. In Matt 5:17 Jesus said,

Matthew 5:17 "Do not think that I have come to abolish the Law or the Prophets; I have not come to abolish them but to fulfill them." (NIV)

There you have it! He fulfilled all the Law and The Prophets along with all the conditions for the promises associated with the names of God. Isn't that exciting! Paul said it this way in 2 Cor 1:20,

2 Corinthians 1:20 "For no matter how many promises God has made, they are "Yes" in Christ. And so through him the "Amen" is spoken by us to the glory of God." (NIV)

Why are all the promises in Jesus yes? Because only through Him are all the conditions to the promises met. Then by us, through Him, the "Amen" (which means let it be so) is spoken. We call God's promises into our lives through His name!

His name is above all of the other names of God because when you speak His name, you are saying all the other names of God together at once. You don't have to remember all the other covenants and the conditions associated with them, because in Christ we have all the conditions met for the promises. You just have to remember the promises and speak the name of Jesus along with them and God's answer is yes! What a thing! There are many promises God has given us in the Bible, it is important to know what these promises are so you can claim them. There are books available that go through the Bible and list all of the promises of God for you, or you can make a note of them as you read your Bible. Either way, it is extremely important to know what they are.

Jesus died on the cross and forgave our sins, now we can come to God knowing that we are made right with Him. We can ask Him for forgiveness for our sins, knowing that we are already forgiven and pure in His sight. I believe Jesus died to reconcile men to God. Would making it harder to have a relationship with God accomplish this? That is why I say that Jesus died to make things simple. He gave us only *two commands* (Matt. 22:36-40),

Matthew 22:36-40 "Teacher, which is the greatest commandment in the Law?" Jesus replied "Love the Lord your God with all your heart and will all your soul and with all your mind. This is the first and greatest commandment. And the second is like it: Love your neighbor as yourself. All the Law and Prophets hang on these two commandments." (NIV)

one commission (Matt. 28:18-20),

Matthew 28:18-20 "Then Jesus came to them and said 'All authority in heaven and on earth has been given to me. Therefore go and make disciples of all nations, baptizing them in the name of the Father and of the Son and of the Holy Spirit, and teaching them to obey everything I have commanded you. And surely I am with you always, to the very end of the age.'" (NIV)

one guide (John 16:13),

John 16:13 "But when he, the Spirit of truth, comes, he will guide you into all truth. He will not speak on his own; he will speak only what he hears, and he will tell you what is yet to come." (NIV)

and one name (Phil 2:9-11),

Philippians 2:9-11 "Therefore God exalted him to the highest place and gave him the name that is above every name, that at the name of Jesus every knee should bow, in heaven and on earth and under the earth, and every tongue confess that Jesus Christ is Lord, to the glory of the Father." (NIV)

to give us everything we need.

Living the gospel is just that, a lifestyle. If you will seek Him and his righteousness—everything that you need will fall into place, exactly like it says in the Bible.

Matthew 6:33 "But seek first his kingdom and his righteousness, and all these things will be given to you as well." (NIV)

Thank you and God Bless!

APPENDIX A

General Tips

❦

Other tips for the courteous gentleman:

When you are assisting with a coat you should hold at her waist level so that she can get her arms into it and then help her slide it up and over her shoulders.

When opening doors for ladies, you should always place yourself on the side that the door hinges. This will keep you from darting in front of them or sticking your arm in their face. Notice that I said when and not if; you should always open doors for ladies.

When you are at a restaurant or other venue, you should always let the lady follow the hostess/usher and you should follow the lady. If there is not a hostess/usher you should lead or walk beside the lady. Also when a lady arrives and leaves from the table, you should stand until she sits, or walks out of sight.

If you are on stairs, you should follow going up and lead going down them. Your mindset for this is you are protecting them from falling.

Dining Tips

When you find something that is unsatisfactory on your plate (i.e. insects or hair), kindly let the waiter know and please do not cause a scene because of it.

Wait until you leave or go to the restroom to remove food from your teeth.

Once all the dishes have been removed, you can then place your elbows on the table.

You can refuse food that has been overcooked or cold, but do so politely.

Cover your mouth (preferably with a napkin) if you are going to cough, burp, or sneeze.

Do not use your silverware as a scoop shovel, piling on all the food possible, rather take small manageable bites (that have been previously cut on the plate) holding your silverware like you would a pen.

Recommended Authors:

Billy Joe and Sharon Daugherty

T.L. and Daisy Osborn

John and Lisa Bevere

Jim Stovall

Tom Leding

Rick Joyner

Lester Sumrall

Kenneth Hagin

James Dobson

John Hagee

Dr. Mark Maynard

Joyce Meyer

www.FireproofMyMarriage.com

www.ReadyToFindGod.com

About the Author

John Buchanan Jr. graduated from Victory Bible Institute in 1999 and then attended Oral Roberts University, graduating with his Bachelor's of Science in Business Administration in 2004. He grew up in Mounds, Oklahoma and currently resides in Broken Arrow, Oklahoma where he is an insurance agent. He has been called to teach on the fundamentals of Christianity, believing that with the Holy Spirit's guidance, they will bring the Body of Christ to the state of holiness necessary for His Glory to once again cover the whole earth. His passion is to see Christians love each other and love the people of this world with the same love that Jesus loved us with.

Be Perfect for Her donates to COTEAM INC. A ministry that sponsors the Good Shepherd Children's Home, An Orphanage Project in Uganda, East Africa.

If you would like to donate or get more information
please contact COTEAM INC at:

COTEAM, INC.
PMB #525
7030-C, South Lewis Ave.
Tulsa, OK 74136-5436, USA

http://tulsa.org/coteam

For more information on our ministries and products, also to view current speaking engagements or request a speaking engagement, visit us at:

www.beperfectforher.com